A Tool Kit

FISHERS OF MEN

JANICE H. GARRETT

www.TrueVinePublishing.org

A Tool Kit for Becoming Effective Fishers of Men
by Janice H. Garrett

Published by
True Vine Publishing Co.
810 Dominican Dr.
Nashville, TN 37228
www.TrueVinePublishing.org

ISBN: 978-1-962783-45-3 eBook
ISBN: 978-1-962783-79-8 Paperback

WHO'S ON YOUR LINE?

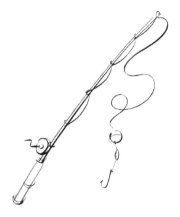

"COME, FOLLOW ME," JESUS SAID,
"AND I WILL SEND YOU OUT TO FISH FOR PEOPLE."
MATTHEW 4:19 NIV

DEDICATION

I dedicate this book to God who is the Originator and Creator of all; Who gave His Son that not only I but all mankind would have the opportunity to accept Him.

In loving memory of our middle son, Robert Allen Garrett II, who saw the good in everyone and shared the love of Christ to those he came in contact with for the Kingdom

To those in need of the Gospel and to those who make themselves available to share the Gospel with those in search of Him.

"For God so loved the world that He gave His only begotten Son, that whosoever believeth in Him should not perish but have everlasting life." John 3:16 (KJV)

SPECIAL ACKNOWLEDGEMENT

A very special "Thank You" to all of my family and dear friends who have supported, encouraged, and prayed for me through this journey. You know who you are. Please forgive me for not listing your names. I pray that the love and respect I have for each one of you will refresh you as you read my note of thanks.

This assignment would not exist without God's Love for mankind, without Jesus giving His life for us, and the help of His Promised Holy Spirit. I am confident that God will see this Evangelistic Tool through to the harvesting of souls.

Wow! What can I say about my loving husband Robert Garrett Sr. but that you are the best! Thank you for believing in me and supporting what you believe God is working in and through me to do of His good will and pleasure. I love you very much!

Born Again Church Ministers In Training instructors and classmates, I love and appreciate the spirit of holiness, excellence, and humility exemplified and taught in class as well as your characters representing Christ outside of the classroom. What a bond!

Bishop Horace and Pastor Kiwanis Hockett of Born Again Church of Nashville Tennessee, words cannot express the love, appreciation, and respect I hold in my heart for you. My prayer is that this tool will represent our Father God and all you have poured, not only into my life and family, but into all who have ever crossed your path. To God be the glory!

My youngest sister Alice Jenkins-Corlew, my biggest fan. Always in my corner pushing and encouraging me forward in all that God has called me to. Because of your genuine love for me as your sister, our friendship, and the unique bond that we have for one another, "I love you and thank God for you daily."

My prayer partners, Dr. Peggy Enochs, Elder Barry, and sister *Cathy Towles*–even when you did not know you were helping birth this tool, your prayers avail much!

My sister, friend, coach, and co-author on the side, Elder Dr. Karynthia Phillips! LOL! "Our labor has not been in vain," declares the Spirit of the Lord. In Jesus' Name, this tool shall accomplish all that the Father God intends!

FOREWORD

I have known the author for more than 27 years and have been profoundly blessed by her devotion to God. Even in the midst of her personal trials, nothing has diminished her love or desire to see His Will fulfilled.

Her fervor to see souls saved is an intense longing of her heart. I highly recommend this practical aid for soul winning. It can be used as a tool by every Born Again Believer to help reach the lost and enjoy the fruits of God's Redemptive Plan. No greater joy can be had than fulfilling The Great Commission of our Lord.

Bishop Horace E. Hockett, Pastor of Born Again Church & Christian Outreach Ministries Founder of Kingdom Builder Network.

TABLE OF CONTENTS

PREFACE

We live in a society that is searching for hope. Christians are in a position to offer hope and salvation to this world. I want to encourage you, my sisters and brothers, to share the Gospel with a strong arm of compassion. You have a unique ability to impact the lives of family, friends, and, yes, strangers.

Our Christian family has a responsibility to serve as first responders to those who have not accepted Jesus as Savior. Individuals who have not accepted Jesus are spiritually dead.

We can assist in resuscitating them by offering the plan of salvation. You have the breath of life in you. Why not share it with those who are dead in sin? I am excited and proud of you for deciding to prepare to win souls for Christ. Yes, you can offer CPR...Christ's **P**owerful **R**edemption.

WHO'S ON OUR LINE?

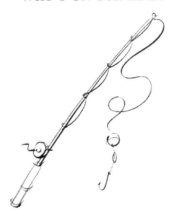

"COME, FOLLOW ME," JESUS SAID,
"AND I WILL SEND YOU OUT TO FISH FOR PEOPLE."

A TOOL KIT
FOR BECOMING
EFFECTIVE
FISHERS OF MEN

INTRODUCTION

"Give Me A Drink"

How many of you have children or have taken care of them when they had to be fed milk from a bottle? If you have, you know that a baby cannot make the bottle for themselves. They need an adult or another mature individual to get it for them; and not just get it for them but get it to the right temperature. A person who is considered an alcoholic believes that they need a drink to help them get rid of their problems. Do we as a Body of Baptized Believers of Christ know when the "lost" are in need of a drink?

Jesus gives us an example of this. Matthew 9:36-37 states "When he saw the crowds, he had compassion on them because they were harassed and helpless like sheep without a Shepherd. Then he said to his disciples, the harvest is plentiful but the workers are few."

The lost (the world) is in need of a "Drink." Some know that they are in need of a drink and some do not know that they need a "Drink." It is our responsibility, the call of the Born Again Believer under the direction of the Holy Spirit to guide them to what they need. When the Samaritan woman came to draw water, Jesus said to her, "Will you give me a drink?" The Samaritan woman said to him, "You are a Jew and I am a Samaritan woman. How can you ask me for a drink?" (Jews do not associate with Samaritan). Jesus answered her, "If you knew the gift of God who it is that asks you for a drink, you would have asked him and he would have given you living water." "Sir," the woman said. "You have nothing to draw with and the well is deep. Where can you get this living water? Are you greater than our Father Jacob, who gave us the well and drank from it himself, as did also his sons and his flocks and herds?"

Jesus answered, "Everyone who drinks this water will be thirsty again, but whoever drinks the water I give him will never thirst. Indeed, the water I give him will become in him a spring of water so that I won't get thirsty and have to keep coming here to draw water." Jesus knew that this woman needed a "drink" that would do more than quench her thirst. Like the alcoholic, their drink is temporary. They will have to keep going back. As we drive around our communities, we see people on corners with signs soliciting money, food, etc. Often we see the same individuals. They seem to have marked that territory. I believe they are saying to us, "Can you see that I am thirsty and in need of a drink?" A refreshing drink that they do not have to thirst for again. Living Water. Water that brings life, healing, and wholeness. I believe they are saying, "I am thirsty now."

What kind of drink do we have to offer the lost?

Let us pray: *Father, in Jesus' Name, we come before You with humble hearts, confessing that we have missed the mark concerning the lives and souls of mankind. We ask that You would, in Jesus' Name, anoint our eyes anew so that we may not only see but also respond according to Your Word to the needs of Your people. You are telling us to open our eyes and look at the field! They are ripe for harvest! We thank You that You are still speaking to us, Your followers, just as You spoke to Your disciples in the past. We look to see where You are working and join You in Your work. We hear You in Your Word, reminding us that the harvest is plentiful but the workers are few. It is our assignment to pray and ask You to send out workers with us into Your harvest field.*

We will go and make disciples of all nations, and we will not become weary in doing good, for at the proper time, we will reap a harvest if we do not give up. We give You glory, honor, and praise for the harvest, in Jesus' Name! Amen.

Matthew 4:19 NIV

CHAPTER ONE

HELP IS NEEDED FOR
THE HARVEST

How long has it been since you intentionally shared the good news of Jesus? It is my desire, through this book, to help you accept the invitation to win souls for Christ. There is a hunger and thirst in the land for the one and only true God. Use your spiritual eyes to see the Father at work in the lives of mankind. Take a moment to see God at work in and through you to do His good pleasure.

John 3:16 KJV tells us, "For God so loved the world, that he gave his only begotten Son, that whosoever believeth in him should not perish, but have everlasting life." So, how do we, as a body of believers, get this Gospel message to God's people? Our love for Christ must stimulate within each of us the desire and obedience to share the blessing of this Great Gospel with others. Jesus promised the disciples, "But you will receive power when the Holy Spirit comes on you; and you will be my witnesses in Jerusalem, and in all Judea and Samaria, and to the ends of the earth," (Acts 1:8 NIV). In other words, we have been given power to witness—to tell someone about the good news, wherever we are in this world. We are called to evangelize. I challenge you to look for opportunities to encourage others to follow Christ.

"Therefore go and make disciples of all nations," (Matthew 28:19 NIV).

The importance of understanding and carrying out personal evangelism requires us to develop a compassionate heart and a love relationship with Christ. We must realize that He suffered the death of the cross for mankind. We are being selfish and could be labeled as "hoarders" when we do not share this gift of salvation with those in need of Jesus Christ. Our love for Christ must ignite within each of us the desire to share the "Gospel of Jesus Christ" with others.

The Bible teaches, "He that wins souls is wise," (Proverbs 11:30 KJV). This book aims to ignite excitement to spread the good news of Jesus and the available gift of salvation. It can be used as a group study for evangelism training and as a resource for personal training in witnessing the Gospel message.

We are all different, and we approach sharing Jesus and witnessing differently, but the Gospel message always remains the same. In Mark 16:15 NIV, we are instructed to "go into all the world and preach the Gospel to all creation." Regardless of how we choose to impact the kingdom of God, there are some foundational guidelines of engagement that assist with our witnessing encounters. No matter whether our encounter is one-to-one, one-to-ten, one-to-one hundred, or one-to-thousands, we need the same basic tools.

Answer the Call to Follow Christ

"Come, follow me," Jesus said, "and I will send you out to fish for people." (Matthew 4:19)

The Bible outlines the importance of becoming fishers of men. Effective witnessing requires that those who have made the decision to follow Christ, with the same love and compassion, compel others to follow Him as well. Before and after the Resurrection, this was a main focus of Christ: to urge those willing to accept and receive this new path. This confirms the significance of reaching the masses. Matthew 4:18-22 NIV, as well as Mark 1:16-20 NIV, show that Jesus' ministry was expanding as He called men to follow Him. These passages teach obedience to the call of Christ to become fishers of men or witnesses. No mention is made of the disciples hesitating, questioning, or making excuses to get out of their new job. The scripture references simply demonstrate Jesus calling the fishermen to train them to become fishers of men. Luke's account of a similar scripture gives more detail in Luke 5:2-11 NIV:

"2 He saw at the water's edge two boats, left there by the fishermen, who were washing their nets. 3 He got into one of the boats, the one belonging to Simon, and asked him to put out a little from shore. Then he sat down and taught the people from the boat. 4 When he had finished

speaking, he said to Simon, 'Put out into deep water, and let down the nets for a catch.' 5 Simon answered, 'Master, we've worked hard all night and haven't caught anything. But because you say so, I will let down the nets.' 6 When they had done so, they caught such a large number of fish that their nets began to break. 7 So they signaled their partners in the other boat to come and help them, and they came and filled both boats so full that they began to sink. 8 When Simon Peter saw this, he fell at Jesus' knees and said, 'Go away from me, Lord; I am a sinful man!' 9 For he and all his companions were astonished at the catch of fish they had taken, 10 and so were James and John, the sons of Zebedee, Simon's partners. Then Jesus said to Simon, 'Don't be afraid; from now on you will catch men.' 11 So they pulled their boats up on shore, left everything and followed him."

This passage is an encouragement and a reminder to be obedient in our witnessing to non-believers of Jesus Christ. Look at each verse and note the disciples' response; Jesus calls and teaches them to become fishers of men.

- ◆ Verse 3: Equipping is essential for the preparation of faith and the miracle power of God.
- ◆ Verse 4: Often, we do not obey God as readily when the request does not seem possible.
- ◆ Verse 5: Doubt is the human response that can be seen in our hesitation and questioning God when obedience requires us to simply launch out.

♦ Verse 5: We can become weary and reluctant to obey God.

♦ Verse 6: God blesses steps of faith.

♦ Verse 7: Covenant relationships with others allow us to share the blessing of the Lord.

♦ Verse 8: Often, remorse and shame overshadow us when the blessings of the Lord are revealed in the midst of doubt.

♦ Verse 9: Obedience reveals God's power for others to see and believe.

♦ Verse 11: Experiences in the natural world prepare us to believe in spiritual breakthroughs in the lives of men as we share Jesus without fear.

Individual Reflection and Discussion

Take a moment to reflect on the above passage pointers again and identify those areas that resemble your experience in preparing to witness for Christ.

1. Are you ready to answer the call?
2. What will make you feel secure in answering the call?
3. What did you learn from the passage?

_____

_____

_____

_____

_____

There is no question that the harvest is plentiful. Look at the media and the various calamities that are occurring all over the world. Look closer at your neighbor or coworker, and see their despair. You have the answer—the hope of Christ—and you can offer salvation to all who are in need.

When the compassion of Christ for mankind becomes alive in us, it births a zeal within to share the provision of salvation with others. Yes, when God's love is made evident through sharing the Gospel, we answer the call to become fishers of men.

Group Reflection and Discussion

Once each person has read the passage several times individually, the facilitator will request you to assemble in groups of 3-4 to discuss the illustration used to portray the moral of the spiritual lesson.

_____
_____
_____
_____
_____
_____
_____
_____
_____

Preparation for evangelism, whether for one-on-one or with large teams, is an ongoing process. The Holy Spirit is at work teaching and guiding us. He leads us to spend time in prayer, Bible study, praise, and worship to further develop the attributes of Christ. It is in those times with Him that we become familiar with His voice and obey as He leads us out into the understanding for deeper things of God.

There is no question that the harvest is plentiful. Look at the media and the various calamities that are occurring all over the world. Look closer at your neighbor or coworker, and see their despair. You have the answer—the hope of Christ—and you can offer salvation to all who are in need.

When the compassion of Christ for mankind becomes alive in us, it births a zeal within to share the provision of salvation with others. Yes, when God's love is made evident through sharing the Gospel, we answer the call to become fishers of men.

Class/Group Reflection and Discussion:

Now when you see this image what comes to mind? Reread the scripture below. Who is on your line?

WHO'S ON YOUR LINE?

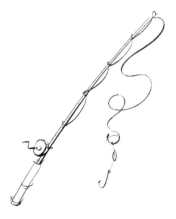

*"COME, FOLLOW ME," JESUS SAID,
"AND I WILL SEND YOU OUT TO FISH FOR PEOPLE."
MATTHEW 4:19 NIV*

CHAPTER TWO
THE HEART TO WIN SOULS
Matthew 9:37-38

37 "Then he said to his disciples, 'The harvest is plentiful but the workers are few. 38 Ask the Lord of the harvest, therefore, to send out workers into his harvest field.'"

The hearts of many are ready to receive Christ. Your family, friends, and even strangers are waiting to be surrounded by the net of compassion as you lead them to Christ in love. Our society is looking for relief from the effects of sin. Think about the escalation of drive-by shootings, home invasions, school violence, domestic situations, gender identity issues, the increase in homelessness, wars and rumors of wars, racism, poverty and terrorist activities all impacting our world. These events are presented by the media as if there is no hope. The good news is we have a hope within us. So, share it. The scripture says, "But in your hearts revere Christ as Lord. Always be prepared to give an answer to everyone who asks you to give the reason for the hope that you have. But do this with gentleness and respect," (I Peter 3:15 NIV).

How can the world hear of His love if we do not share the Gospel? How can the world believe or have faith in God? In Romans 10:17 HCSB, the scripture reminds us, "So faith comes from what is heard, and what is heard comes through the message about Christ." So go, tell somebody! Many say we do not have to go door-to-door knocking and passing out tracks anymore to share Jesus. The lost and those who want God have tele-evangelists, webinars, Internet Bibles, and other electronic mediums on their smartphones, tablets, and laptops. None of these methods take the place of God's people sharing the love of Christ face-to-face with others. Jesus came all the way from heaven to share Himself with the world. Surely, we can leave the comforts of our homes to do the same.

The church must be careful not to adapt to the latest fads of our society. We must be wise, always reminded that we are not to succumb to the strategies of Satan to distract us from Kingdom building. I am not against technology, but we must physically communicate with people as often as we can.

Look at I Corinthians 9:19-23:

"For though I am free from all men, I have made myself a slave to all, so that I may win more. 20 To the Jews I became as a Jew, so that I might win Jews; to those who are under [a]the Law, as under [b]the Law though not being myself under [c]the Law, so that I might win those who are under [d]the Law; 21 to those who are without law, as without law, though not being

without the law of God but under the law of Christ, so that I might win those who are without law. 22 To the weak I became weak, that I might win the weak; I have become all things to all men, so that I may by all means save some. 23 I do all things for the sake of the Gospel, so that I may become a fellow partaker of it" (NASB).

It is important that we maintain a heart that is pure which will always keep us in tune to God's leading. Living a life of holiness enables us to respond to the concerns of mankind, as we let our light shine in the midst of adversity or jubilee. Consider the following verses:

"Let your light so shine before men, that they may see your good works, and glorify your Father which is in heaven,"(Matthew 5:16 KJV).

"For God so greatly loved and dearly prized the world that He (even) gave up His only-begotten (unique) Son, so that whoever believes in (trusts, clings to, relies on) Him shall not perish-come to destruction, and not be lost-but have eternal (everlasting) life. For God did not send the Son into the world in order to judge -to reject, condemn, to pass sentence on-the

world, but that the world might find salvation and be made safe and sound through him," (John 3:16-17 AMP).

The Lord moved by His Spirit upon the heart of His Son to give His life that all mankind might be saved. As believers in Christ, we have embodied that same unconditional love that will allow the Holy Spirit of God to move upon us and lead us to those in need of salvation? Take time to examine your heart, your relationship with God, and your lifestyle as a Christian to be sure you are representing Christ with a pure heart. When we serve man without guilt or shame, our effectiveness of winning souls for Christ increases.

We must examine our hearts to assess whether we have the compassion as Christians to reach out to the lost for Christ. It is my heart's desire that we, as born again believers, allow the love of God that has transformed us, to drive us with an earnest desire to pay our experience forward. Allow others the opportunity that we have had to repent and accept Jesus Christ as Lord and Savior of our lives and live a life of victory.

The connection within us established by an intimate relationship with the Father, sparks a passion for the unsaved and those headed for destruction. The souls of the lost become top priority. Many years ago I experienced an example of urgency. My phone rang and when I picked it up to answer there was a sound of an alarm and a recording that said intrusion alarm. There was an urgency within me that something serious was about to happen. I took it as if there was about to be an attack on the country and we needed to take cover. I realized my family was not in our apartment with me. I opened the door and began to look for them to tell them about the alarm. I wanted to encourage them to quickly come inside, so that we were all together and prayerfully safe.

During the search for my family, I noticed everything about my surroundings appeared to be normal. My heart and my spirit was at peace knowing that all was well with my family and our community. As I quietened myself and sat down, I pondered a few questions and I am now posing them to my readers. Can you imagine having the opportunity to share the Gospel with the lost only to have something tragic happen and you did not follow through? How would you feel? The heart of the Father desires that none would perish. He has given us an assignment to go and fish people out of troubled waters bringing them to a safe shore.

The devil desires to steal, kill, and destroy our loved ones, neighbors, and others. He attempts to accomplish this by intruding in their lives with material gain, deception, and other strategies. Intrusion is defined as "an illegal act of entering, seizing, or taking possession of another's property." The devil's plan is to violate the rights of God's people by bringing substitutes that are temporary and that will not provide them salvation.

Each day we must practice evangelism or what I call *intrusion prevention.* Sure, many may feel unworthy, nervous, or insecure about witnessing. What is the barrier that inhibits or delays you from casting out the lifeline–that is, sharing the "Good News?" Help is on the way. During an empowerment session known as "BOSS Training" (under the direction of Al and Hattie Hollingsworth), I learned to implement the REPOH rule in my life in various situations. *REPOH* is an acronym which stands for *Repetition, Easy, Pleasure, Often,* and *Habit.* Actively practicing the REPOH rule in preparation for evangelism can assist with building confidence when participating in soul winning, and to help witnessing become like second nature.

REPOH

Repetition: Each day, *repeatedly* see where God is working in the life of another and join what He is already doing.

Easy: Practice, practice, practice and witnessing will become *easy* for you.

Pleasure: As you witness daily, witnessing will become *pleasurable* for you; when something is easy for you to accomplish, it becomes a pleasure.

Often: Share the good news *often.* When an experience is pleasurable, you will do it often.

Habit: Actively sharing the Gospel with others becomes a *habit* for you.

REPOH

Repetition: Daily recite scripture

Easy: Practicing verbally, scripture daily, it will become easy during recall

Pleasure: Repetition and recall, builds confidence and relaxes you as you please God

Often: Meditate, review and recite several times

Habit: The more that you practice, the scripture will become part of you

We must capture opportunities as God places them before us. Be consistent when witnessing; Witness! Witness! and Witness! In St. John Chapter 4, we read about a Samaritan woman who came to draw water from Jacob's well where she met Jesus. Jesus was at the right place at the right time. Because of his genuine love and compassion for God's people, He was able to witness truth to this woman; which caused her to make a decision to become an effective witness for the kingdom of God. You are an ambassador for Christ. Soul winning is an honor and should be a pleasurable experience. Training for success is key to evangelism. During the process of developing your skills to evangelize, the feeling of inadequacy and robotic motions will decrease. The natural sharing of the Gospel should not become a tradition or a routine, but a sacrifice from a genuine heart to win the lost.

It is very important that during preparation for sharing the Gospel you understand that everyone does it differently. God has designed all of us to impact others specifically for the Kingdom. Witnessing cannot be approached with the idea that one style fits all. Remember that God has chosen you to be the one to share with a specific person. Only you will be able to reach that person's heart in your special way. God wants to share His love through you with that particular person. Our personalities, passions, and gifts are uniquely packaged to reach someone who perhaps has never been to church or has strayed away for one of many reasons. For example, a homeless person or your employer may have distanced themselves from the church but each one needs to be reminded of God's love.

In other words, we all have an assignment and how it is carried out varies. The tools that are in this book are to give you support and guidance as you approach launching a life of sharing the good news of Christ. It is important to understand that salvation is personal and each individual person expresses his/her relationship with Jesus Christ differently. There is no question that, at the end of the day, we must all repent and accept Jesus into our lives. Jesus says, "I am the door. If anyone enters by Me, he will be saved, and will go in and out and find pasture," John 10:9 (NKJV). How do we lead others on this journey of hope? How do we lead them into the door of life?

Individual Reflection and Discussion:

1. What is your current feeling about witnessing?
2. Whose responsibility is it to witness? (i.e., only pastors, ministers)
3. What do you experience when you hear bad news affecting our society? What can you do?

_____

_____

_____

_____

_____

Groups: Reflection and Discussion

1. How has God commissioned us to stand in the gap for the lost in order to disrupt the activity of the devil (enemy) and stop the intrusion of the souls of mankind? Suggestion: Live godly among humanity and offer hope as you let your light shine and encourage others to accept Christ. Sharing the good news offers a solution to mankind for the intrusion of souls.

_____

_____

_____

_____

_____

WHO'S ON YOUR LINE?

"Come, follow me," Jesus said,
"and I will send you out to fish for people."
Matthew 4:19 NIV

CHAPTER THREE

BARRIERS THAT HINDER EFFECTIVE WITNESSING

If we want people to attend a party or special event, what do we do? Most of us would send out an invitation. Evangelism is just like sending out invitations to potential guests about a party. There will be some who accept the invitation and others who will decline the invitation. Similarly to the invitation of Christ, one will either enter or decline a relationship with Christ Jesus. Do not be disappointed. Some of us are responsible for planting the seeds of faith, and others water those seeds, but it is the Lord who knows when it's exactly the right time for people to respond and enter the Kingdom. As Paul stated, *"I planted the seed, Apollos watered it, but God has been making it grow," (I Corinthians 3:6 NIV).*

Regardless of the role we play in the life of the new Christian candidate accepting the invitation—planting, watering, or bringing in the harvest—we have a part. Rejoice and pray for those coming into the Kingdom. I Corinthians 3:5-9 discusses the roles Apollos and Paul played in evangelism. "What, after all, is Apollos? And what is Paul? Only servants, through whom you came to believe—as the Lord has assigned to each his task. I planted the seed, Apollos watered it, but God has been making it grow. So neither the one who plants nor the one who waters is anything without God, who makes things grow. The one who plants and the one who waters have one purpose, and they will each be rewarded according to their own labor. For we are co-workers in God's service; you are God's field, God's building" (NIV).

Take a moment and read Matthew 9:10-11 MSG.

"Later when Jesus was eating supper at Matthew's house with his close followers, a lot of disreputable characters came and joined them. When the Pharisees saw him keeping this kind of company, they had a fit, and lit into Jesus' followers. "What kind of example is this from your Teacher, acting cozy with crooks and riffraff?"

Have you ever had an experience like this? What did you do? The people to whom you are witnessing may not look like you, think like you, or smell like you. The goal is to invite them into a life-changing relationship with Jesus. Sure, even your friends may not understand your zeal as you intentionally begin to share the good news and implement the tools gleaned from this book. Stay the course of preparation to winning souls. Remember that this book is a tool to assist either your personal evangelism or a group of people out evangelizing the community. As Christians, we are to invite others into the Kingdom. The invitation to salvation is deliverable in many ways: conversation, a tract that is distributed, or an email. There are other methods that the Holy Spirit will use to guide you to successfully share the Gospel.

Ultimately, we want the person you are talking with to desire and accept the gift of salvation as you lead them to Christ. Do not be afraid to share. II Timothy 1:7 tells us, "For God did not give us a spirit of timidity, of cowardliness, of craven and cringing and fawning fear-but, (He has given us a spirit) of power and of love, of calm and well-balanced mind, discipline and self – control," (Amplified). You are not alone. The following scriptures are also great encouragement for us as we get started in our evangelism efforts:

"If you live in Me (abide), vitally united to Me (abide), My words remain in you and continue to live in your hearts, ask whatever you will and it shall be done for you," John 15:7 (Amplified).

"Lean on, trust and be confident in the Lord with all your heart and mind, and do not rely on your own insight or understanding," Proverbs 3:5 (Amplified).

"For all have sinned and fall short of the glory of God," Romans 3:23 (NIV).

The five barriers listed below are often common when beginning to witness.
Fear

When we allow our human emotions to control us, we are prevented from trusting the empowerment of the Holy Spirit to help us. We are actually denying God's power to work in us and for us. In order to effectively witness to the lost, we cannot be cowards. Unbelievers do not want to be called cowards, and surely as born again believers we do not want to be identified as such either.

As we continue preparing to be more effective witnesses, we must take an honest look at our spiritual and daily lives. If we find that we are fearful, we have to allow ourselves to trust the work of the Holy Spirit that is alive within us. We can combat fear by earnestly getting into the presence of God. We enter His presence by worshiping Him in song, reading and meditating on His Word, and praying. In short, we are strengthened by "building up [ourselves] on [our] most holy faith," Jude 1:20. Then it is time to move out, not in our own self-assurance, but in the confidence of God's Holy Spirit. What excitement awaits as we watch God bless our witnessing through the number of people who accept the invitation to salvation.

"There is no fear in love; perfect love casts out fear," I John 4:18a (NKJV). The commentary notes suggest that possessing God's love results in fearless confidence toward God and love for the brethren.
So here is a question: do we love our brethren? Is there a

true compassion or concern for the lost? If not, we are walking in the sin of omission, for the Great Commission tells us "to go into all the world and preach the Gospel to every creature," (Matthew 16:15 (NKJV).

Rejection

There are times when rejection feels very embarrassing if the candidate is rude, loud, poking fun, or not receiving what we are offering to them. If any of these behaviors occur, it is imperative to not take it to heart. That person is rejecting Christ, not us. Jesus was rejected for sharing the Gospel. This Gospel actually offered new life. Jesus' focus was the will of the Father concerning those who were lost in sin. I Timothy 2:4 (NIV) clearly speaks to God's will that all people be saved and to come to a knowledge of the truth. When rejection does rear its ugly head, we can do as Mark 6:11 teaches and shake the dust from our feet. Even so, we ought to pray for the candidate, remembering someone will water if we plant the seed and it is God that makes it grow (I Corinthians 3:6 NIV).

Insufficient in Bible Knowledge

Whether we have been Christians for years or recently began the Christian journey, we will always desire to know more about the Bible. To fulfill that longing, we can memorize scriptures and keep a reference or note card in our Bible. It is also a good idea to highlight scriptures on salvation or the new life in a particular color, for example: red representing the blood of Christ, and green-new life. As we thumb through the Bible, we can easily locate passages on these subjects.

Heart Check!

Empty out all barriers. Let the mind of Christ be in you so that you can do the will of the Father in the earth. Philippians 2:5 (KJV) suggests, "let this mind be in you, which was also in Christ Jesus," (KJV). Each one of us is on divine assignment by the Holy Spirit. Wherever He is working, join Him.

Lack of Trust

We must have confidence in the greater One who lives and dwells inside of us. Every day we must build ourselves up in faith and rely on the word of God. It is the truth needed in preparation to win the lost. Remember, you are an instrument being used by the Almighty God. Trusting God requires that we rely on what we do not see. Learn to have confidence in the power of His Word, for God declares in *Hebrews 13:5b, "I will never leave you nor forsake you."*

Somewhere along the way, you learned to believe, depend on, or trust the words of a loved one. You learned to trust what that person said. For example, when your dad or granny taught you how to ride your new bike, you trusted that if you did what you were told, you would not be allowed to fall. *Proverb 3:5 says, "Lean on, trust in, and be confident in the Lord with all your heart and mind and do not rely on your own insight or understanding," (AMP).*

Our heavenly Father who has all power and authority promised that His presence will always be with us. So what do we have to fear? And where should our confidence be? Our confidence must be in the role of the Holy Spirit. Jesus, promised in *John 14:16 (NIV), "and I will ask the Father, and he will give you another advocate to help you and be with you forever."*

Cultural Barriers

A blind spot that is often overlooked by the body of Christ is how often we are only concerned about our own culture or socio-economic group. Additionally, we can be so self-focused that we sometimes ignore or even shun the many souls who are members of other cultures. Be reminded that God holds each of us accountable to offer the invitation of hope to any and every one. Our world is huge and the invitation is for everyone. We cannot refuse to offer the plan of salvation because of our differences. God's example of giving His only Son for all humanity is the perfect example of love for diversity. *"For God so loved the world that He gave His one and only Son, that whoever believes in Him shall not perish but have eternal life" (John 3:16).*

There are many people whose hearts God has softened and prepared to receive His Gospel message. Are we missing those people due to our self-centeredness and disobedience? We must be careful not to operate with a me-myself-and-I mentality. We must eliminate all self-ishness. Yes, Prejudices. When we received salvation and became born again, the old us was cleansed. We each have been made new by the shed blood of Jesus Christ at Calvary. We have to stay focused and remember that all have sinned and we all have fallen short of the glory of God, (Roman 3:23).

The primary solution to demolishing barriers to evangelism is the individual's personal relationship with God. Allowing the power of The Holy Spirit to work in and through us frees us to offer to anyone that which we have freely received. We are charged to "cure the sick, raise the dead, cleanse the lepers, drive out demons. Freely (without pay) you have received, freely (without charge) give," Matthew 10:8 (AMP).

The Help of the Holy Spirit

What better way to get help with your barriers than from the Holy Spirit. Consider meditating on the following passages:

"And I will ask the Father, and He will give you another Comforter (Counselor, Helper, Intercessor, Advocate, Strengthener and Standby) that He may remain with you forever, The Spirit of Truth, Whom the world cannot re-

ceive (welcome, take to its heart), because it does not see Him, nor know and recognize Him. But you know and recognize Him, for He lives with you (constantly) and will be in you," John 14:16-17 (AMP).

"Having therefore obtained help of God, I continue unto this day, witnessing both to small and great" Acts 26:22a (AMP). "But ye shall receive power, after that the Holy Ghost is come upon you: and ye shall be witnesses unto me both in Jerusalem, and in all Judea, and Samaria, and unto the uttermost part of the earth," Acts 1:8 (KJV).

"But you shall receive power (ability, efficiency and might) when the Holy Spirit has come upon you; and you shall be my witnesses in Jerusalem and all Judea and Samaria and to the ends (the very bounds) of the earth," Acts 1:8 (AMP). "But you will receive power when the Holy Spirit comes on you; and you will be my witnesses in Jerusalem, and in all Judea and Samaria, and to the ends of the earth," Acts 1:8 (NIV).

Effective soul winning requires the Holy Spirit being alive and active in our lives. It is stated that He is our Helper and that He will abide with us forever. As our natural vehicles require gas to get us from one place to another, our spirits needs a fresh infilling each day by His spoken word and through God's presence living inside of us. This filling will keep us in tune with the souls that the Father would have us witness to daily as he leads us. The Holy Spirit has come and is the empowerment that we must have to win the loss.

Are You Ready?

My question to you is the same question that Paul asked some disciples who he found in Ephesus in Acts 19:2: "Did you receive the Holy Spirit when you believed?" (Acts 19:2 NIV). They answered, "No, we have not even heard that there is a Holy Spirit." What is your answer to Paul's question? If you answered as those Ephesians did, then receive the empowerment of God's Holy Spirit *now* in Jesus Name!

Another useful solution is to step out in faith and try your hand at witnessing. Some say practice makes perfect. Studying or participating in training helps alleviate some of the pressure you feel when you share the Good News. There will naturally be times that barriers like discouragement and disappointment will resurface. These barriers will try and serve as roadblocks to your attempts to witness, but persevere. Keep trying!

Exercise

Play soft music, quiet your spirit, and then read the passage below. Take time to journal and discuss what you hear God saying in the following passage from Jude 1:17-22 (NIV): "But, dear friends, remember what the apostles of our Lord Jesus Christ foretold. They said to you, "In the last times there will be scoffers who will follow their own ungodly desires. These are the people who divide you, who follow mere natural instincts and do not have the Spirit. But you, dear friends, by building yourselves up in your most holy faith and praying in the Holy Spirit, keep yourselves in God's love as you wait for the mercy of our Lord Jesus Christ to bring you to eternal life,"

Catherine Marshall in one of her inspirational writings made our assignment as disciples clear when she said, "Our commission is quite specific. We are told to be His witness to all nations. For us, as His disciples, to refuse any part of this commission frustrates the love of Jesus Christ, the son of God."

Also, Jesus' original commission is quite clear and specific. "Go, therefore, and make disciples of all nations, baptizing them in the name of the Father and of the Son and of the Holy Spirit, teaching them to observe everything I have commanded you. And remember, I am with you always, to the end of the age," Matthew 28:19-20 (HCSB).

_____

_____

_____

_____

_____

_____

Janice Garrett

Reflection and Discussion:

Discuss barriers to witnessing with which can cause a struggle. I have listed several to get you started:

*Fear
*Shyness
*Inadequate education
*Cultural difference
*Lacking scriptural knowledge
*Feeling of unworthiness.
*Add any additional barriers you feel.

Think through how fear and how lack of trust can inhibit or prevent you from witnessing? What measures can be taken to resolve these barriers?

For Groups

Allow members of the group to share some of the barriers of their struggle? Then allow group members to suggest with constructive remarks and critiques some ways to break through those barriers.

_____
_____
_____
_____
_____

WHO'S ON YOUR LINE?

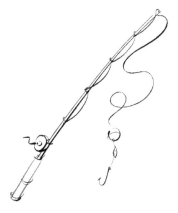

"Come, follow me," Jesus said,
"and I will send you out to fish for people."
Matthew 4:19 NIV

CHAPTER FOUR

SHARING THE GOOD NEWS: THE PLAN OF SALVATION

Since this book is an instructional starting point for those interested in witnessing and a reminder of our responsibility to witness, let us be sure we have a scriptural understanding of the plan of salvation. I have provided a few scriptural references to get you started. As you acquire more scriptures, you will be able to add them to your tool box.

When you approach someone to share the Good News of Christ, be gentle as you offer new life to the individual. Our society consists of people of different religious and cultural backgrounds so keep in mind perceptions will vary; therefore, to ensure success, the key is to listen to the guidance of the Holy Spirit as you begin witnessing. Listen closely to the gentle voice of God for direction when initiating conversation.

You want to be sure the person to whom you are talking understands that Jesus died for his/her sins and is the door into heaven. The key to the door is repentance and accepting the gift of forgiveness for sin. The simplicity of salvation can be complex to unbelievers, primarily because Satan wants to keep them confused (blind). Mathew 10:7 (CSB) says, *"As you go, announce this: 'The kingdom of heaven has come near.'"*

Patience and assurance from the scriptures will offer

comfort and support for both of you. There may be cases when the person is unsure why he/she must be born again. The following scriptures should help you clear up this uncertainty.

Start with Romans 3:23 (KJV) which says, *"For all have sinned, and come short of the glory of God."* We have all been born naturally into sin because of Adam and Eve's behavior in the Garden of Eden (Genesis 2:15-25 and 3:1-22). In order to enter heaven, the sin nature in which we were born must be removed by a process of repenting and accepting forgiveness. In other words, we must make the exchange—our old nature for a new one—made possible by the work of Jesus Christ on Calvary. That exchange is activated by our repentance of sin, and acceptance of Christ into our heart.

In this chapter, you will be presented with two different scriptural approaches as tools to assist you in presenting the Good News. First is the Romans Road to Salvation, which is a collection of scriptures from the book of Romans that has a step- by-step method you can follow. Second is a series of scriptures in the book of John. You might want to highlight these scriptures in your Bible, write them on index cards, or memorize them to give you more comfort in conversation.

As a student of the Word, you will develop skills that will help you discern which scriptures and methods you should use with each individual. As you share God's word with someone, please remember to pray and ask the

Holy Spirit for guidance. Also pray that the people's hearts are being prepared for the hope of salvation. Think on the following scriptures for more encouragement:

"For God did not send the Son into the world in order to judge-to reject, to condemn, to pass sentence on the world; but that the world might find salvation and be made safe and sound through Him," John 3:17 (AMP).

Because if you acknowledge and confess with your mouth that Jesus is Lord (recognizing His power, authority, and majesty as God), and believe in your heart that God raised Him from the dead, you will be saved. For with the heart a person believes (in Christ as Savior) resulting in his justification (that is, being made righteous-being freed of the guilt of sin and made acceptable to God); and with the mouth he acknowledges and confesses (his faith openly), resulting in and confirming (his) salvation (Romans 10:9-10 AMP).

"For the wages of sin is death, but the free gift of God is eternal life in Christ Jesus our Lord," Romans 6:23(AMP).

"I came that they may have and enjoy life, and have it in abundance—to the full, till it overflows," John 10:10b (AMP).

Think back on your own salvation experience.

Where were you when you repented of your sins and accepted Christ into your life? What was going on in your life at the time? Who prayed for you? In what way was this a life-changing experience? God will place people in our path who will have similar experiences that we have had, and there will be those whose experiences will differ greatly. It is imperative that we are sensitive to the leading of the Holy Spirit when ministering salvation to the lost. Remember that He does the work in their hearts. We are merely the instruments from which they will hear the Gospel. Jesus says, "And I, when I am lifted up from the earth, will draw all people to myself," John 12:32 (NIV).

Exercise:

Role Play Lifeline Plan A:

With a partner, pray the following prayer of salvation. Role play the following scenario as person one leads the prayer to receiving salvation and person two responds.

Person One:

Father in Jesus' name, I thank You for drawing _____ (add name) to You. Your Word tells us that Your Son, Jesus Christ died for each of our sins and we believe Your Word. So we join today with _____ in prayer as (he or she) confesses their sins and asks you for forgiveness. Lord, You said in Your Word (the Bible) that if we confess our faults (sins) that You are faithful and just to forgive us and cleanse us from all unrighteousness (sin).

Person Two Repeat After Person One:

Lord, I confess my sins and I am sorry. I ask You to forgive me and cleanse me of my sins. I ask You to come into my heart. Thank You for forgiving and cleansing me from sin.

Person One: (Depending on how you are led by God, you can add the following :)

We know that we need help to live a life that brings honor and glory to Your name, so we ask You in the precious Name of Jesus, that You would give us the gift of Your Holy Spirit.

Holy Spirit, take control of my life. Lord, I accept Your Holy Spirit in my heart by faith. I love You and thank You that I am forgiven of my sins - born again and filled with Your Spirit.

In Jesus Name, Amen.

It is important to ask your new sister or brother if someone can follow up to assist with this new birth or salvation experience. Let the person know you will continue praying for him/her. Encourage the person to attend church to learn more about Christ and this new life. Help them to see the need for the guidance and leadership of a pastor or shepherd in the spiritual growth and maturity of any believer. Remember the church is a good source for education and fellowship with Christian sisters and brothers. As stated in scripture: *"How good and pleasant it is when God's people live together in unity" (Psalm 133:1 NIV)*

Don't stop meeting together with other believers (Hebrews 10:25a). Healthy relationships are important for the spiritual growth and development of all Christians. Explain to the new believer the importance of having support, spiritual guidance, and accountability. You can say something like the following:

"How exciting! Your family size has just increased to include every Christian in the world. You will need the strength, support, and encouragement of your new family to walk out this Christian journey. We encourage you to quickly connect with a local church that teaches and preaches the full counsel of God's Word."

The body of Christ is strengthened when we unite in corporate worship, praise, and prayer. Being new in Christ, you are now of this body and have rights and privileges as a born-again believer. Satan does not want this and will do everything within his power to encourage you to live outside of the will of God by keeping yourself isolated from these corporate activities. So stay connected! Being connected to a church family and other believers of like faith will keep you in the place of accountability that we all need. It becomes a built in accountability system designed by our Heavenly Father.

As you study and meditate on the Word of God, keep these scriptures dear to your heart:

Not forsaking or neglecting to assemble together [as believers], as is the habit of some people, but admonishing (warning, urging, and encouraging) one another, and all the more faithfully as you see the day approaching," Hebrews 10:25 (AMP).

"How good and pleasant it is when God's people live together in unity," Psalm 133:1 (NIV).

It is very important that new believers understand they cannot pay money for salvation nor work off their sin. Show them, if they will allow, that salvation is by grace through faith.

Ephesians 2:8-9 (NKJV) says, "For by grace you have been saved through faith, and that not of yourselves; it is the gift of God, not of works lest anyone should boast" (NKJV).

Role Play Lifeline Plan B:

This is a basic lesson of having a person admit sin and ask for forgiveness. In this example, the candidate learns to confess (speak) with his/her mouth and believe that God gave His Son to die for his/her sins. Forgiveness is a lifeline. Once one accepts the lifeline, he /she is removed from the pool of those drowning in guilt and shame. Forgiveness saves you from an eternal life of torment. How? The result of acknowledging your sin, asking for forgiveness, accepting Christ in your heart, and by believing you are forgiven, results in salvation. It is why we say that you are saved. Jesus is the Lifeline.

Romans 10:13 (ISV) says, *"Everyone who calls on the Name of the Lord will be saved."*

Basic ABC to Salvation—Plan C:

Look at the Roman Road to salvation, which offers a basic ABC to salvation. God demonstrated love for the world while we were in sin (See Romans 5:8).

A - Acknowledge that we have sinned and ask for forgiveness (See Romans 3:10, Romans 3:23, and Romans 6:23a).

B - Believe Jesus Christ is your Lord and Savior and accept Him (See Romans 10:13).

C - Confess Jesus Christ as Lord and accept that you are a new creation (See Romans 10:9).

There will be times individuals will be very emotional because of immoral acts committed in the past and have accepted a spirit of condemnation and shame. In these cases, you will want to take more time sharing additional scripture references providing the person proof of forgiveness. Please do not become impatient. Witnessing can require sacrifice more time than you expected, especially when you are laboring to birth a new life into the Kingdom of God. Because of this, you will find more scriptural help below:

"Therefore, since we have been made right in God's sight by faith, we have peace with God because of what Jesus Christ our Lord has done for us," (Romans 5:1 NLT).

"So now there is no condemnation for those who belong to Christ Jesus," (Romans 8:1 NLT).

"And I am convinced that nothing can ever separate us from God's love. Neither death nor life, neither angels nor demons, Neither our fears for today nor our worries about tomorrow—not even the powers of hell can separate us from God's love. No power in the sky above or in the earth below—indeed, nothing in all creation will ever

60

be able to separate us from the love of God that is revealed in Christ Jesus our Lord," (Romans 8:38-39 NLT).

"Therefore, he is able to save completely those who come to God through him, because he always lives to intercede for them," (Hebrews 7:25 NIV).

Scripture Memorization

Listed here are scriptures you should know when witnessing, and tips you can use during this time of training:

Highlight these scriptures in your Bible particular color. Label the pages on which you find these scriptures with a colorful sticky note or tab.

"For God so loved the world, that he gave his only begotten Son, that whosoever believeth in him should not perish, but have everlasting life," (John 3:16 KJV).

"For the wages of sin is death; but the gift of God is eternal life through Jesus Christ our Lord," (Romans 6:23 KJV).

"For God sent not his Son into the world to condemn the world; but that the world through him might be saved," (John 3:17 KJV).

Available in the back of this book are Fishing for People Scripture Memory Cards you can take along or highlight in your Bible. Also available in the back of the book are scriptures on love, peace, encouragement, and doubt.

Basic Terms Used When Witnessing

It is important to communicate clearly when witnessing. Try to be familiar with their language and culture. Terminology should not be taken lightly because everyone did not grow up in church or in a Christian environment. Make sure you can effectively define terms we often take for granted. Do not assume the candidate knows what you mean. Feel free to rewrite the following definitions (without changing the meanings) so they are clear enough for you to explain.

Love – to have a strong affection for; a strong caring for
God – The "Elohim" God; Our Sovereign Creator and Ruler of heaven and earth
Jesus – The Son of God; The Anointed One; Messiah, Savior
Sin – willful disobedience to the instructions of God's Word
Repent – to have sorrow for action and turn from that action toward God
Confess – admit or acknowledge something; declare
Believe – to put confidence or trust in

Salvation – deliverance or preservation from harm, ruin, or loss; deliverance from sin and its consequences

Born Again – spiritual rebirth; regeneration

Holy Spirit – The third Person of the Trinity; the Triune God sent as another means of help, comfort; Teacher; Comforter

Carnal – fleshly; bodily pleasures or appetites

Flesh – physical nature of mankind

Perish – to suffer complete destruction or ruin

Eternal Life – always or forever living

Forgive – to pardon; to relieve or release

Witness – to testify or respond

Transgression – a violation of a command; a breaking away from authority

WHO'S ON YOUR LINE?

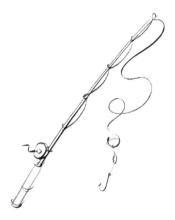

"Come, follow me," Jesus said,
"and I will send you out to fish for people."
Matthew 4:19 NIV
Matthew 4:19 TNIV

CHAPTER FIVE

HELP FOR THE JOURNEY:
THE HOLY SPIRIT, DISCIPLESHIP, AND INTERCESSION

The Holy Spirit

On any journey, it is always good to have someone walk along with you. New converts will want to know they are not alone. It is important that they understand the Holy Spirit is present to guide, comfort, and help them on this new spiritual rebirth as a Born-Again Believer; what a new life journey! During your time with new converts, be sure they understand that there is no reason to be afraid of God's Holy Spirit. People often have misconceptions of the purpose of the Holy Spirit based on past experiences, schools, and other teachings as if He is evil or something demonic. For example, like the impression they may have internalized about spirits from television shows. Teach the new convert that the Holy Spirit is The Spirit of God. He is gentle and to be reverenced. The Holy Spirit is a helper, a guide, and a companion for Christians.

One of the ways to be sure *they* understand the work of the Holy Spirit is to be sure that *you* are clear about the work and presence of the Holy Spirit in your personal life. The Spirit of God begins working once any new convert accepts Jesus, and He will continue working as each of us develops an intimate relationship with Him. The infilling process has different names or expressions.

The process can be called the Holy Ghost and fire, the presence of God, or being baptized with the Holy Ghost. Converts may be asked, "Have you been filled with the Spirit since you believed?" (As referenced in Acts 19:2a). These are all ways Christians talk about the infilling of the Holy Spirit.

Discipleship and Follow Up:

The primary assistance you can provide for the people you are to disciple includes prayer, support, and encouragement for them to become affiliated with a spiritually healthy community of believers. You want to encourage them to join a church (fellowship) so they can be nurtured by a pastor and loving members who live godly lives. Always display a nonjudgmental attitude. Use precautions to prevent handicapping your new brothers and sisters in Christ. We do not want to stunt growth or make them dysfunctional Christians by playing the role of the Holy Spirit, or lording our own opinions over them during this new journey.

Keep a smile, relax, and maintain boundaries. You don't want to be so close in their space that you both are uncomfortable. Focus on encouraging them in this new life. New converts will come to understand that salvation does not make them perfect. They will have times of discouragement and probably a sense of failure. At times, they will actually make mistakes. Remind them that they can repent and start over immediately.

Your tool box must contain instruments to leave with the new converts so they can contact you or your ministry for further assistance. Take time to familiarize yourself with the instruments in your tool kit so you can explain them fully. There should be, for example, a pamphlet known as a "tract" that will reassure the new Christians of the reality of the salvation they have recently received. Also include a resource list for church services in your community and other affiliate churches. Contact information for these ministries will be helpful as well.

If your ministry decides to obtain demographic information for follow up, remind the converts that they will receive a call, email, or a letter in the mail in a few days. If possible, determine the best time to contact them to follow up.

Intercession:

To God be the Glory! How does it feel to be fulfilling the Master's assignment according to Matthew 28:19 to go make disciples? According to the Strong's Concordance, the Hebrew word for "make" is "bara" (baw'raw') which means "to create, shape, form, fashion, or something new." II Corinthians 5:17 (NLT) reads *"...anyone who belongs to Christ has become a new person. The old life is gone; a new life has begun!"* As disciplers, we have been given an ordained assignment by God. We are in partnership with the Holy Spirit, walking alongside the new believers in intercession and encouragement.

Think about your prayers of intercession as if you are a midwife coaching mothers-to-be in the labor and delivery room. The midwife requires experience and knowledge of their role to coach the success of the delivery. In the same way, your prayers assist in the new believers' birth and growth as Christians. New converts need your prayers. Although it may not be possible with everyone you witness, whenever it is possible, try to develop a close enough relationship so you can be specific in prayer depending on the needs of the individual. Remember how you felt when you began this new walk with the Lord. You felt like a new baby needing help from others. Pray that the lives of these individuals would be fashioned and shaped according to the Word of God. You literally become their earthly advocate by offering support and encouragement as they grow in the grace and knowledge of who God says that they are.

This assignment is not to be taken carelessly. The maturity of these people and their destiny lie within your faith in the Word of God and your consistent and fervent prayers. Your assignment is to approach heaven on the behalf of each convert until God releases you from this responsibility. Intercession will not be by your prayers only; the example of the life that you will live before them will be an act of intercession as well. Don't focus only on what the natural eye will see, but seek the Holy Spirit concerning the will of the Father for each convert. Each day, week, month, and year will be different for each person and so will your prayers. Before the journey begins, I encourage you to ask the Holy Spirit for help in keeping your heart, mind, and spirit ready for this God-sized mission.

WHO'S ON YOUR LINE?

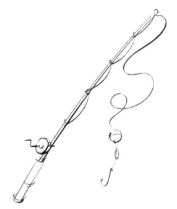

"Come, follow me," Jesus said,
"and I will send you out to fish for people."
Matthew 4:19 NIV

Ministry Planning Checklist

Preparation				
Planning Checklist Items	Yes	No	Not Required	Comments
Complete training				
Seek area assignment from leader				
Begin praying for assigned location with team members				
Team set time at least 2-3 times a week to pray for members and family				
Pray for receptive hearts, minds, and spirit of the individuals in your assigned area				
Execution (personal or in groups in the community)				
Implementation Planning Checklist	Yes	No	Not Required	Comments
Confirm Meeting Location				
Ensure you have all necessary materials needed for witnessing				
Assign responsibilities to each team member. Suggest 3-4 members per group				
Pray before and after outreach				

Debriefing and follow up				
End of the day Checklist Items	Yes	No	Not Required	Comments
Return all materials to their location				
Determine follow-up meeting when date is decided to go and witness				
Review and Log data				
Determine follow up and discipleship				

Fishing For People Scriptures

And I will ask the Father, and He will give you another Comforter 9Counselor, Helper, Intercessor, Advocate, Strengthener, and Standby), that He may remain with you forever. John 14:16 AMP

But you will receive power when the Holy Spirit comes to you. Acts 1:8a TNIV

For God so loved the world that he gave his only begotten Son, that whosoever believeth in him should not perish, but have everlasting life. John 3:16 KJV

For the wages of sin is death, but the gift of God is eternal life in Christ Jesus our Lord. Romans 6:23

And they were all filled with the Holy Spirit and began to speak with other tongues, as the Spirit gave them utterance. Acts 2:4 NKJV

In the same way, the Spirit helps us in our weakness. We do not know what we ought to pray for, but the Spirit himself intercedes for us through wordless groans. Romans 8:26 TNIV

Fishing For People Scriptures

The Spirit of Truth, whom the world cannot receive (welcome, take to its heart), because it does not see Him or know and recognize Him. But you know and recognize Him, for He lives with you (constantly) and will be in you. John 14:17 AMP

And he asked them, Did you receive the Holy Spirit when you believed (on Jesus as the Christ)? Acts 19:2a AMP

For God sent not his Son into the world to condemn the world; but that the world through him might be saved. John 3:17 KJV

The thief comes only to steal and kill and destroy; I have come that they may have life, and have it to the full. John 10:10 TNIV

And do not be drunk with wine, in which is dissipation; but be filled with the Spirit. Ephesians 5:18 NKJV

Trust in the Lord with all your heart and lean not on your own understanding; in all your ways submit to him, and he will make your paths straight. Proverbs 4:5-6 TNIV

SCRIPTURES OF LOVE, PEACE, ENCOURAGEMENT, AND DOUBT

Love

- ♦ God Is love. I John 4:16 NIV
- ♦ Love covers a multitude of sins. I Peter 4:8 NIV
- ♦ Love must be sincere. Romans 12:9 NIV
- ♦ Love is patient, love is kind. It does not envy, it does not boast, it is not proud. It is not rude, it is not self-seeking, it is not easily angered, it keeps no record of wrongs. Love does not delight in evil but rejoices with the truth. It always protects, always hopes, always perseveres. Love never fails. I Corinthians 13:4-8a NIV
- ♦ Greater love has no one than this: to lay down one's life for one's friends. John 15:13
- ♦ Dear friends, let us love one another, for love comes from God. Everyone who loves has been born of God and knows God. I John 4:7
- ♦ Be completely humble and gentle: be patient, bearing with one another in love. Ephesians 4:2
- ♦ And now these three remain: faith, hope, and love. But the greatest of these is love. I Corinthians 13:13
- ♦ Jesus replied; Love the Lord your God with all your heart and with all your soul and with all your mind. Matthew 22:37

- ◆ The second is this: Love your neighbor as yourself. There is no commandment greater than these. Mark 12:3

Peace

- ◆ You will keep in perfect peace those whose minds are steadfast, because they trust in you. Isaiah 26:3 NIV
- ◆ Peace I leave with you; my peace I give you. John 14:27a NIV
- ◆ Let the peace of Christ rule in your hearts, since as members of one body you were called to peace. And be thankful Colossians 3:15 (NIV)
- ◆ Peacemakers who sow in peace reap a harvest of righteousness. James 3:18 NIV
- ◆ Mercy, peace and love be yours in abundance. Jude 1:2 NIV
- ◆ Make every effort to keep the unity of the Spirit through the bond of peace. Ephesians 4:3 NIV
- ◆ Now may the Lord of peace himself give you peace at all times and in every way. II Thessalonians 3:16a NIV
- ◆ How beautiful on the mountains are the feet of those who bring good news, who proclaim peace. Isaiah 52:7a NIV

Encouragement

- ◆ But encourage one another daily. Hebrews 3:13a (NIV)

- Encouraging, comforting and urging you to live lives worthy of God, who calls you into his kingdom and glory. I Thessalonians 2:12 (NIV)
- Wherefore comfort yourselves together, and edify one another, even as also ye do. I Thessalonians 5:11 KJV
- Come unto me, all ye that labour and are heavy laden, and I will give you rest. Matthew 11:28 KJV
- I will lift up mine eyes unto the hills, from whence cometh my help. My help cometh from the Lord, which made heaven and earth. KJV
- Be on your guard, stand firm in the faith; be courageous; be strong. I Corinthians 16:13 NIV
- What shall we then say to these things? If God be for us, who can be against us? Romans 8:31 KJV
- Let every one of us please his neighbor for his good to edification. Romans 15:2 KJV
- Strengthening the disciples and encouraging them to remain true to the faith. Acts 14:22a (NIV)

Doubt

- Jesus replied, truly I tell you, if you have faith and do not doubt, not only can you do what was done to the fig tree, but also you can say to this mountain, Go, throw yourself into the sea, and it will be done. Matthew 21:21 (NIV)
- Stop doubting and believe. John 20:27b (NIV)

- But when you ask, you must believe and not doubt. James 1:6a (NIV)
- Trust in the Lord with all thine heart, and lean not unto thine own understanding. Proverbs 3:5 KJV
- But let him ask in faith, nothing wavering. James 1:6a KJV
- And Jesus answering saith unto them, Have faith in God. Mark 11:22 a KJV
- Now faith is the substance of things hoped for, the evidence of things not seen. Hebrews 11:1 KJ

SUPPLEMENTAL TOOLS FOR USE WHEN EVANGELIZING

SORRY WE MISSED YOU
DOOR HANGERS

FOLLOW-UP COMMUNICATION FORM

Name: _____

Address: _____

_____

Contact Information:

Home Phone: _____

Cell Phone: _____

Work Phone: _____

Emergency Contact Name: _____

Emergency Contact Phone: _____

Facebook: _____

IG: _____

X: _____

Birth date: _____

Place of Birth: _____

Favorite Food or Restaurant: _____

Favorite Color: _____

What do you most enjoy doing?

_____

_____

Prayer Request: _____

_____

_____

COMMUNICATION DATA CARD

NAME:_____   DATE: _____

PHONE: _____   ADDRESS: _____

CITY: _____   STATE: _____ ZIP:_____

SEX: (M) (F)   MARRIED ( )   SINGLE ( )   BIRTH DATE: _____

EMAIL_____

CANDIDATE CHURCH NAME:_____

RECEIVED: SALVATION ( )   BAPTISM OF THE HOLY SPIRIT ( )   HEALING ( )   RECOMMITMENT ( )

OTHER ( ) _____

COMMENTS: _____

_____

_____

CERTIFICATE OF SALVATION

THIS CERTIFICATE IS AWARDED TO

Today I have openly declared that Jesus is Lord and believe in my heart that God raised Him from the dead, and the Bible says that I am saved.

_____
Signature

_____
Date

Therefore, if anyone is in Christ, the new creation has come: The old has gone, the new is here! II Corinthians 5:17 (NIV)

84

CERTIFICATE OF COMPLETION

THIS CERTIFICATE IS AWARDED TO

_____

"Come, follow me," Jesus said, "and I will send you out to fish for people."

Matthew 4:19 NIV

_____
SIGNATURE

_____
DATE

_____
SIGNATURE

_____
DATE

About the Author

Janice Garrett is a Senior Elder of Born Again Church and Christian Outreach Ministries in Nashville Tennessee under the leadership of Bishop Horace and Pastor Kiwanis Hockett. She serves under the Pastoral Care Ministry of her church, a teacher, and gifted intercessor with a passion for caring for her family and friends, as well as God's people. Janice is a graduate of Nashville State Community College where she earned a Child Development Associate Credential; and Technical Certificate in Early Childhood Education. She holds an Administrative Credential from Tennessee State University, and a BS degree in Ministry from Immanuel Bible College. In July 2020, Janice completed courses and received certification from the American Association of Christian Counselors for Caring for People God's Way in Christian Counseling. Janice's love for humanity has no boundaries as is evident in her work as an Early Childhood Professional for over 40 years. She has been the director of a Child Development Center for over 23 years. Her compassion, creativity, and hope lies in not just seeing her infants, toddlers, and pre-school-age children develop into healthy "little people," but also in seeing them grow in their relationship with Christ. This book is a reflection of the sincerity of her heart as she seeks to nurture and equip both the believer and the non-believer with the necessary tools to be educated, develop and mature as 21st century Christians.

Janice is the daughter of the late Alice and Harry Jenkins and the wife of her loving, supportive, and faithful husband Robert Allen Garrett Sr. Married for over 43 years, she and Robert reside in Antioch, TN. They have four children: DeAnthony Sr., *LaShonda* (deceased), *Robert II* (deceased, to whom this book is dedicated), and Daniel; a daughter in-love Erica; and four grandchildren, Jazmone, Kyndal, DeAnthony II, and Jaiden. Janice enjoys cooking, shopping, fellowshipping with family and friends, spending time in worship and being a servant in her church body as the Lord allows.

Printed in the USA
CPSIA information can be obtained
at www.ICGtesting.com
LVHW010407100924
790285LV00003B/11